MW0092894ɔ

31 Prayers for
Single Christian Women

Navigating The Waiting Season With Prayer And Purpose

This book belongs to:

_____

Table of Contents

Introduction:

Jesus instructs us to ask, seek, and knock in order for the door to be opened. Maybe you've been knocking for a long time, praying that the Lord would send you a spouse. Or perhaps you've grown weary and have stopped asking altogether. Any and all time spent in prayer is meaningful, and we know that with the Lord, nothing is wasted! However, have you considered setting aside a specific time daily to pray over your singleness and for your future?

As a single woman who desires marriage, it's essential to include God in the process. These prayers are designed specifically with you in mind, to bring you closer to the Lord by exposing your heart to Him. He will comfort, uplift, and strengthen you! From praying for guidance on dating to confessing when you've been disappointed by relationships, God wants to hear from you. Allow this time spent in prayer to mold you and your relationship with Jesus.

When we pray, we come to the Lord in faith! These prayers won't just focus on your desire for marriage; they will keep your eyes set on the Giver of good things. God is more than able to go above and beyond your requests. He gives us singleness as a time to rely on Him and build trust. As you remain patient and hopeful, watch how the Lord molds your heart through prayer!

Trusting God's Timing for Relationships

"Wait on the Lord: Be of good courage, and He shall strengthen thine heart: wait, I say, on the Lord."

Psalm 27:14

Dear Lord,

Sometimes, patience is a struggle. Throughout Scripture, You remind me to wait on You, and at times, this feels challenging to do. It's hard not to notice others receiving the relationships, marriages, and families my heart desires. I repent for focusing on my own timeline, knowing Your timing is always perfect.

God, help me to surrender to You when I struggle with comparison. Grant me the strength to resist jealousy and envy. You have a unique plan crafted for me, and I shouldn't compare my life to others. I want to walk in courage, recognizing the many blessings You've given to show Your faithfulness. Help me to rejoice in Your gifts instead of dwelling on what I haven't received. Teach me to find joy in every season of life, knowing You only give what is good and withhold when it isn't the right time.

Father, I choose now to settle my heart. You tell me that in You, my heart can be strong. I want to trust in Your perfect timing, believing that You aren't holding out on me. What You have in store is worth the wait! Help me to fix my eyes on Jesus, who endured the cross for the joy set before Him. He trusted in Your perfect timing, and so will I! In Jesus' Name, Amen.

Reflection:

Use this area to continue praying or record your thoughts and/or questions prompted by the previous prayers.

Overcoming Loneliness and Isolation

*"Turn thee unto me,
and have mercy upon me; for
I am desolate and
afflicted. The troubles of my
heart are enlarged: O bring thou
me out of my distresses."*

Psalm 25:16-17

Heavenly Father,

You know the depths of my heart. Nothing is hidden from You. Thank You for knowing me inside and out and still loving me. Because You are a good Father, I know that You desire to care for every part of me. I don't have to hide my emotions or fears from You.

Lord, I lay my feelings of loneliness at your feet. You know that I desire a spouse to share life with—someone to love through the highs and lows. Sometimes, singleness feels so isolating. But Jesus, I know that You are a man of sorrows, acquainted with grief. You know what it's like to be lonely. You carried burdens that no one else could understand, and I'm sure that felt isolating at times. Yet You tell me that I'm never alone because You are with me. Help me find comfort in Your presence. While I pray for a godly husband, I don't want to wait for that person to bring me comfort because I know that You are the true comforter of my soul. In You, I have all I need for today.

God, help me to love You in the midst of my suffering and despair. When my heart is heavy, You say that Your burden is light. Lord Jesus, let the joy of the Lord be my strength as I allow You to draw me near in times of loneliness. Help me to delight in Your fellowship!
In Jesus' name, Amen.

Reflection:

Use this area to continue praying or record your thoughts and/or questions prompted by the previous prayers.

Navigating the Pressure to Marry

*"Let us then approach
God's throne of grace with
confidence, so that we may receive
mercy and find grace to help us in
our time of need."*

Hebrews 4:16

Holy Father,

You tell me in Scripture that I can approach You with boldness. For each moment, You give me the grace and mercy that I need. So, Lord, I come to you today asking for wisdom.

Father, there is so much pressure to marry from friends, family, and culture. Singleness is almost looked down upon as if it were a sin. The idolatry of romantic love is everywhere.

Jesus, I know that You lived a life of singleness and You were complete because You lived for Your Father's will and glory. Help me to also keep my eyes fixed on my true purpose in life– to love God and glorify Him. As I do this, Lord, will You help my singleness to be a testament to Your faithfulness to me?

May Your goodness overflow in me and show others that Your love is what all other loves stem from. Scripture says that You are love itself! Being loved by You is the highest form of love I can experience. Help me to be in awe of how You lavish Your love on me and others.

I take joy in how much You love me, Lord. Your love casts out fear! I choose to not be afraid of what people think of me and to not allow myself to doubt Your goodness. In Jesus' Name, Amen.

Finding Contentment in Singleness

"Not that I speak in respect of want: for I have learned, in whatsoever state I am, therewith to be content."

Philippians 4:11

Lord Jesus,

Your Word says that I can be content in every circumstance. Yet there are times when contentment in my waiting season is particularly challenging when my heart desires a relationship. Lord, You tell me that I can do all things through Christ who strengthens me— and that includes singleness! I want to believe that when You say *all*, you truly mean *all*! I know that I can be content here and now because I trust Your Word.

Help me not to be dragged down by a spirit of discontentment. I want to live with gratitude in my heart. So, Lord, thank You for your provision. You have given me every spiritual blessing in Christ. Your "yes" is always for my good, and your "no" is always for my good.

Lord, I trust that right now, You have allowed me to be single for a reason. I trust in Your provision and that You withhold no good thing. I believe that You give me what I need, not necessarily what I want. I know You're a good Father.

Help me to not covet what others have, Lord. Guide me away from anxiousness about what I don't have and into thankfulness for what I do. I know through Your strength, I can be content in every circumstance, even here. In Jesus' Name, Amen.

Dealing with Disappointment in Relationships

"Hope deferred maketh the heart sick: but when the desire cometh, it is a tree of life."

Proverbs 13:12

Dear Lord,

My heart can be heavy with disappointment at times. I've longed for a spouse but have not yet found the right person. Despite my best efforts, I haven't been able to enter a relationship that leads to a lasting marriage.

But God, I know that this burden is not one I'm meant to bear. You, Lord, are the One who directs my path. Help me to trust You for my future.

Father, forgive me for moments when I've indulged in self-pity and complaining. Holy Spirit, help me turn to You when I feel disappointed and allow You to comfort me. Your truth and grace are a balm to my weary soul.

Jesus, I know that You have experienced disappointments—far more than I have. Train my heart to be resilient and focused on seeking Your kingdom first, not my own. You show me what it's like to truly live in fullness. Help me remember that fulfillment isn't found in a person, boyfriend, or husband—but in God. If I only keep my eyes on what I don't have, I'll fall prey to a sickness of the heart. Lord, help me focus on what is eternal and find true satisfaction in You.

When I face disappointments in my dating life, Lord, I pray that they will push me closer to You and not away from You. I will not lean into despair because my true hope is in You. May all my experiences be the fuel that shapes me more and more into the image of Your Son. In Jesus' Name, Amen.

Balancing Independence and Dependence

"Trust in the Lord with all thine heart; and lean not unto thine own understanding. In all thy ways acknowledge him, and he shall direct thy paths."

Proverbs 3:5-6

Heavenly Father,

Your Word tells me not to lean on my own understanding. Your ways are not my ways; Your thoughts are not my thoughts. You are infinitely more patient, wise, and merciful than I could ever imagine. No wonder You tell me to trust You. You not only have perfect insight into my life, but You love me. You want the best for me. And what I *imagine* as my best could be different from what You *know* is my best. Lord, help me to rely on You for guidance. Help me not to jump to conclusions on what actions to take to reach my end goal. I want to be led by You.

In Proverbs, it says that You'll direct my path. But to direct my path, it means I have to be moving! So God, as I take steps forward, would You help me to grow in discernment? Lord, when I'm considering who to go on dates with, help me to use the wisdom You have given me and not my own intellect. I don't want to be independent of You when I make these choices.

Lord, I know that feelings can easily blur clear vision. Help me to stay grounded in You, level-headed. I don't want to trust my own understanding. Instead, I put my confidence in You, knowing You'll lovingly lead me through it all. In Jesus' Name, Amen.

Coping with Rejection and Heartbreak

*"The Lord is nigh unto
them that are of a broken
heart; and saveth such as be
of a contrite spirit."*

Psalm 34:18

Dear Jesus,

There are times when being single can feel challenging, and rejection can be especially hard. It's easy to wonder if being single means something is wrong with me or if love will ever come.

Lord, You know what it's like to face rejection. You were scorned by family, friends, and the people You came to save. You were betrayed by a close friend. You are close to those who are brokenhearted because You fully understand.

I know my value does not come from others' actions or their love. I don't need a man's love to know I am worth loving. You created me, died for me, and are with me every day—I am infinitely cherished. Lord, help me let go of looking to others for validation. Help me feel loved by You, Lord. I want to believe that I am precious to You, even when it's hard to feel it in my heart. Would You draw me close?

God, I don't want to become bitter or lean into self-pity. I want to honor You with my thoughts and actions. Please guide me to truth and understanding as I navigate feelings of rejection and heartbreak. I lay down any unforgiveness, jealousy, or pride right now. Keep my heart soft to hear and obey. In Jesus' Name, Amen.

Managing Sexual Temptation

*"Flee fornication. Every
sin that a man doeth is without the
body; but he that committeth
fornication sinneth
against his own body."*

1 Corinthians 6:18

Dear Lord,

Nothing is hidden from Your sight. You know my every thought. Even the things I wish no one knew—You know, and still, You've stayed with me.

Lord, You know that sexual temptation is a common struggle. Our world is oversaturated with sexually driven content in song lyrics, TV scenes, and movie plots. It sometimes feels nearly everywhere I turn, making it challenging to avoid the effects.

But Jesus, You taught us what it means to be truly human. I am not at the mercy of instinct. Your Word tells me to flee from sexual immorality and use self-control. Any sexual gratification outside of marriage is a sin not only against You but against the body You've given me. I want to be a good steward of my body, the temple of the Holy Spirit.

I want to stop this sin before it starts, so Lord, help me deny sexual content access to me. Help me skip scenes and stop songs when they start to involve things of a sexual nature. I want to help my spirit grow in purity through the power of Your Spirit.

I know that all sin starts in the mind. And Jesus, You said that even what we think about can be sin. Help me not to excuse a thought simply because it's a thought. I want to be aggressive against anything that threatens to come between my love for You. Remove any desire in me that seeks to gratify my flesh and exchange it with a desire to love You above all else! In Jesus' Name, Amen.

Setting Boundaries in Dating

*"Keep thy heart with
all diligence; for out of it are
the issues of life."*

Proverbs 4:23

Lord God,

I recognize the importance of boundaries in cultivating healthy relationships. Help me establish boundaries concerning my time, physical touch, and emotions. Grant me wisdom in these areas, knowing that my decisions are rooted in my heart. May my heart remain focused on You, prioritizing Your kingdom above all else.

In my time, Lord, I pray that You will help me to have focus. It's so easy to just do whatever feels good in the moment. Sometimes that can mean giving someone too much access to me too soon. It's also very common to use someone for their attention, without realizing that I genuinely want their heart. Help me not to play games. I know that You are the one who gives me every breath! So help me, Jesus, to turn my time over to Your leadership. I pray that I will be sensitive to how You want me to use it.

In my touch, Jesus, I need firm guards in place. I do not want to be proud. I do not want to assume that I am above sin and temptations. Help me to preemptively avoid placing myself in situations where I can compromise. I don't want to fall into sin with my body. Please guide me as to what standards I need to set. And then, Holy Spirit, would You help me to keep them?

In my emotions, Father, I need to guard my heart. When I get excited, it's easy to want to imagine a life with someone and enjoy all the butterflies that come with a love interest. But I don't want to get ahead of myself and cause unnecessary heartbreak. I need self-control to not overly pour my emotions into a situation or person. Help me to be sensitive each step of the way. In all these, God, I trust You. Amen.

Handling Criticism from Others

*"The Lord is on my
side; I will not fear: what can
man do unto me?"*

Psalm 118:6

Heavenly Father,

There are moments when I sense scrutiny from others. Those on the outside looking in can make comments on my looks, past relationships, and my singleness. At times, I find myself vulnerable to these opinions. Lord, grant me the strength to cultivate resilience and let unkind judgments roll off me. I aspire not to harbor bitterness but to transcend it.

You reassure me that You stand by me. I need not fret over human judgments. My foremost concern should be whether my actions align with Your will. If they do, the rest becomes inconsequential. Your Word illuminates the path of righteousness and meaningful connections. Help me distinguish those who convey Your wisdom from those who do not. My ears are attentive solely to Your voice.

I trust that Your timing holds purpose. My present single status is part of Your unfolding plan, which demands my attention. May I stay focused on what You have ordained for me now, disregarding external pressures. Thank you, Jesus, for sustaining and elevating me through every circumstance. In Your Precious Name, Amen.

Dealing with Comparison and Envy

*"But let every man prove
his own work, and then shall
he have rejoicing in
himself alone, and not in
another."*

Galatians 6:4

Dear Lord,

I know comparison is the thief of joy. Yet, it is so easy to fall into. Scrolling through social media can feel like an endless maze. At so many turns, I see happy couples going on cute dates, getting engaged, and throwing beautiful weddings. Lord, I yearn for what they have, sometimes questioning why it hasn't come to me in my time. I confess that envy is wrong. It only eats away at my heart and brings me no closer to my desires.

I want to be happy for others and not feel like I'm lacking because of what they have! Jesus, root out anything causing bitterness in my soul. I believe in Your goodness and love for me. I know that You will provide for me in your timing, and that I shouldn't be comparing my timeline to others. Your timing is perfect.

I want to feed my spirit with truth so that when the temptation to envy comes into my mind, I can fight it off with Your Word. You tell me that freedom is found in You. I am accountable for my actions, and I want those actions to speak of trust in my Father. Someone else's victory isn't my loss. My value does not decrease with another's blessings. I refuse to fall prey to comparison as a child of God. Lord, I choose to step away from the lies of the enemy and step into Your wisdom and light.
In Jesus' Name, Amen.

Building Self-Confidence and Self-Worth

*"I will praise thee; for I
am fearfully and wonderfully
made: marvellous are thy works; and
that my soul knoweth right well."*

Psalm 139:14

Father God,

Women are so quickly defined by the titles we hold in our society. Often, the title "wife" seems to be emphasized as having greater value. As a single woman, it's easy to feel less than, as if those who are married are living out their purpose more fully. God, I know that my value doesn't stem from these roles. I don't need a spouse to prove my worth. Lord, help me to believe this in moments of doubt.

With age and personal insecurities, there can be fears about my attractiveness and my ability to attract a husband. While I want to take care of my appearance, I know that true beauty is much more than physical. You give me the opportunity to become more like Your Son, Jesus, who is the source of all beauty. As I trust in You and am shaped by You, I will radiate with His likeness. You alone give me value and worth, and I should rejoice in how You have made me.

Lord, help me to build my self-image on what You say about me. I don't want to tear myself down because of beauty standards that don't really matter. I want to be beautiful in Your eyes, Lord. Your opinion matters most! Thank You for making me so wonderfully! In Jesus' Name, Amen.

Understanding God's Plan for Marriage

"For this cause shall a man leave his father and mother, and shall be joined unto his wife, and they two shall be one flesh."

Ephesians 5:31

Father God,

Love is often depicted in movies as butterflies, fireworks, and heart-racing moments. Though I desire to have a passionate and exciting romance, I also want to be rooted in You and what You say about marriage. Marriage is hard work. It's an image of Christ's love for the church. It's a sanctifying process that I know will involve dying to my flesh in order to care for, respect, serve, and love my husband.

Lord, help me not get swept up in the fantasy. I don't want to chase a feeling that will lead me to disappointment. I want to love someone for who they are, with Your eyes, Lord. Help me to be discerning and not follow after someone because they give me a rush. Marriage is most beautiful when it is Your design, Father. I want a relationship that glorifies You and builds Your kingdom.

Lord, would you prepare me for my spouse? Help me to learn compassion, selflessness, and good communication. I want to improve where I can, God, so that I can enter a relationship and be a healthy partner. Expose things in my heart that need to be removed and areas that need growth. Help me to be sensitive to Your Spirit leading and guiding me into maturity. Help me to also grow in humility and learn from good marriage examples around me.

Lord, I trust in Your design and Your timing for my marriage. In Jesus' Name, Amen.

Surrendering Control to God's Will

*"A man's heart deviseth
his way: but the Lord directeth
his steps."*

Proverbs 16:9

Dear Lord,

There are times when I may be tempted to take control away from You. There are times when I may even want to force a relationship to happen, simply because I'm tired of waiting. Oh Lord, help me to surrender control to You. I know the danger involved when I try to take the wheel. I know that only Your timing and plans are perfect. I don't need to hold on so tightly. I want to be free to move with Your Spirit.

While I'm single, Lord, would you help me to focus on Your will for me here and now? I don't want to waste my time. My life, ministry, and purpose will not begin the day I meet my husband. I am presently able to walk in my calling as Your child and messenger on earth. I know You want to shape and grow me. Help me to be open to Your leadership. In my work, Lord, give me wisdom to know what decisions I need to make. In my finances, God, help me to be faithful and a good steward. With my time, I surrender my attention to You and where You want me to invest.

Lord, I give You full access to direct my life. I refuse to be bitter when things don't go my way because I trust Your leadership. I relinquish control to You, the Good Shepherd. In Jesus' Name, Amen.

Facing Cultural Expectations

*"And be not conformed
to this world: but be ye transformed
by the renewing of your mind, that ye
may prove what is that good, and
acceptable, and perfect, will of God."*

Romans 12:2

Oh Lord,

Cultural expectations can be such a burden at times. There seems to be a deadline for all the important milestones: getting married, owning a home, and having a stable career, all by a certain age. Lord, you tell me not to conform to this world. I don't need to set my values or expectations based on my culture's pressures. I also don't want to think like the world.

Jesus, I need You to transform my mindset concerning these matters. I don't want my vision of marriage to be what the world defines it as. I want my desires to be grounded in Your Word. If I follow the world, I won't be drawn to the right relationship. Guard my thoughts when they go away from Your expectations for my future marriage.

In my financial expectations, Lord, help me to not exalt money. This world worships finances. I don't want to be a slave to anything except righteousness. Please help me not to give into fears about the future, because You are my provider. I trust You to care for me, Lord, with or without a spouse.

In my career and work, lead and guide me where You want me to be. I want Your presence to saturate every part of my life and be a light for You. Help me not to feel pressured to be at a certain level or have a specific title in order to judge my success. Success is serving and loving, You Lord.

Lord, I pray that You will continue to shape me and help me not be molded by the world's expectations.
In Jesus' Name, Amen.

Healing from Past Relationships

"Remember ye not the former things, neither consider the things of old. Behold, I will do a new thing; now it shall spring forth; shall ye not know it? I will even make a way in the wilderness, and rivers in the desert."

Isaiah 43:18-19

Heavenly Father,

When I reflect on past experiences, it's challenging to feel completely healed. Memories still carry a sting, and I understand Your guidance not to dwell on the past, yet I need Your help in moving forward.

Lord, it's so easy to try to numb the pain with distraction. Whether it's scrolling through social media, watching hours of mindless TV, or staying constantly busy, I don't want to run away from the healing that needs to take place just because I think it will be a painful experience. Father, You love me. Do what You must to heal the hurt in my soul.

I don't want the hurt from my past to negatively influence my future relationships–from my friends to my family, I will choose to open my heart to healing to protect those whom I now love and will love in the future. Lord, give me wisdom as to how to move forward and ease this pain. I want to follow Your leadership and be sensitive to the Spirit.

I will focus my attention on how You have the power to make even the dry seasons beautiful. Your Word says You make streams in the desert—abundance out of nothing! God, in the places of my heart that haven't seen peace and fruitfulness, would You provide Your living water? I refuse to allow dwelling on the past to make me bitter or discouraged about the future. I serve a God of miracles who can provide me with all I need. I choose to trust You, Lord! In Your Name, Amen.

Finding Purpose and Fulfillment

"For I know the thoughts that I think toward you, saith the Lord, thoughts of peace, and not of evil, to give you an expected end."

Jeremiah 29:11

Dear God,

Sometimes people talk about marriage as the moment when true life begins. But, Lord, I don't want to sit idly because I'm single. I don't want to pause on plans because I'm afraid certain choices will stall my marriage from happening. I believe that You have a plan for me in this season of my life. You've used singles all throughout Christian history and in Scripture. I know that my life can be fulfilled and purposeful right now! Jesus, You tell me that the greatest commandment is to love the Lord, my God, and to love others as myself. I know that You have provided all I need to live in fullness!

Father, help me to reject thoughts that You don't care for me because You haven't brought me a spouse. These are lies to distract me from my calling and all that You have for me. I refuse to be ineffective in ministry because I'm waiting on marriage. I will keep running this race because I know that Your actions are good for me. Your thoughts aren't to ruin my life by keeping me single, but to bring peace, hope, and joy. I know that in You, I am complete. Although I greatly desire a husband, Lord, I will love You first. I'm always on Your mind. You tell me that Your thoughts about me outnumber the grains of sand on the beach (Psalm 139:18)! I'm not forgotten, and I am fully loved.

You have equipped me to live as a kingdom citizen, sharing the gospel and living in Your love. Today I declare that I will not be slowed down by singleness but allow You to use it for Your purposes! In Jesus' Name, Amen.

Cultivating Patience in Waiting

"To everything there is a season, a time for every purpose under heaven."

Ecclesiastes 3:1

Dear Lord,

The earth teaches me patience. There is a time to plant and a time to reap a harvest. But in between, there's waiting. At times, it seems I've been waiting for something I can't fully see, but Lord, I know that You're growing something beneath the surface. The waiting can be so hard because all I see is ground; I can't see the seed that is growing. However, I know that You hear my prayers and that You love me. God, I'm believing that while I'm waiting, You're preparing something in me and in my future husband that we will need.

Lord, I pray that You will strengthen me in the meantime. Increase my patience. I don't want to rush the process when You're making something beautiful. The worst thing I could do is uproot what's been growing before it's ready to harvest. Help me to not be premature with my actions. I want to rely on the Spirit to keep my heart steady. I believe that You'll strengthen me as I turn to You.

Though I can't see anything happening now, Lord, I will use my spiritual eyes to discern. You tell me to have courage, and I choose to not be a victim of fear. I know that whenever You bring my spouse, it will be the perfect time. You will care for me! I don't need to be anxious. I choose peace in Your safety and truth.
In Jesus' Name, Amen.

Strengthening Faith Amidst Doubt

*"And straightway the
father of the child cried out, and
said with tears, Lord, I believe; help
thou mine unbelief."*

Mark 9:24

Lord Jesus,

I bring my fear and hesitation to You, acknowledging that my struggle at times to pray for a spouse is rooted in a lack of trust and faith that You'll answer my prayer. You tell me in Your Word to ask and keep on asking, and yet there are times that I struggle to pray with boldness. So Lord, I'm choosing to come boldly before You now with what my heart desires, and I trust that You will answer accordingly.

Help me pray in faith for my future husband. It's challenging to keep praying when it feels like nothing is happening, but I know You perform miracles and love to display Your goodness and power when there seems to be no other way.

I know that You love me. You withhold nothing good from me. I'm trusting and believing that I will have a husband that I can serve You with. I want a man of God who will care for me and whom I can respect and follow. I want to reflect Your love for the church through my marriage. I believe that with a husband who loves You, I'll be able to run my race in a unique way that will show the world Your goodness. Lord, this is the desire of my heart. Help me to have faith in You to fulfill it.
In Jesus' Name, Amen.

Embracing Singleness as a Gift

"For I would that all men were even as I myself. But every man hath his proper gift of God, one after this manner, and another after that."

1 Corinthians 7:7

Lord Jesus,

I know You were single, yet You were whole. Paul told the Corinthians that he wished they could all be single. Lord, though I want to be married, help me not to scorn singleness. In singleness, I have more time to devote to You. I want my heart to be wholly set on serving You with all of me. Direct me to those who I can minister to and the special ways You have orchestrated ministry opportunities that I can fulfill. Help me to see areas where I am effective *because* I'm single.

I'm choosing to believe Your Word, that You use each of us uniquely, and that singleness is given as a gift. I'm going to run my race with passion because I love you, Jesus! I want to use my singleness to further Your kingdom, like Paul and John the Baptist. I am strong and given all the tools I need to be successful in my life because I'm equipped with the Spirit.

No matter how long my singleness lasts, I want my heart set on You, Lord. I want to be ready in season and out of season for whatever You have for me, and to take joy in You! Help me to stoke the fire in my heart for You and to show the world that in singleness, the Lord is good to me. I refuse to be hidden; I'll be a light on a hill. I want to share Your goodness with those around me and be effective for Your kingdom. I choose to believe that right now, my singleness is *good* and an intentional gift from You. In Your Name, Amen.

Resisting Unequally Yoked Relationships

"Be ye not unequally yoked together with unbelievers: for what fellowship hath righteousness with unrighteousness? and what communion hath light with darkness?"

2 Corinthians 6:14

Dear God,

Your Word plainly states that I am not to be unequally yoked. While nonbelievers can have good personalities, good looks, and offer good chemistry, if they don't love you, Lord, I know I can't partner with them in a romantic relationship. The world tells me it's not a big deal, and that as long as they respect my beliefs, that's good enough. God, I want to believe what Your Word tells me; that light cannot dwell with darkness.

Help me to trust that by following Your Word, I am on the best path for my life. As I walk in obedience, Holy Spirit, I ask that You help me guard my heart. I don't want to flirt with this temptation. Help me to establish clear boundaries that would keep me from giving into my emotions when I'm faced with an attractive option that isn't a believer.

God, I know my actions stem from my heart. Help my heart to love You first and foremost. You tell me that if I love You, I'll obey You. Help me to love You with this sacrifice, knowing that satisfying You is better than satisfying myself.

May my personal standards for dating reflect Your goodness to those I encounter. I want my life to be a testament to how much You mean to me! Your glory is my delight, and though the sacrifice doesn't come easy, I wouldn't want to give You something cheap. Help my obedience be a costly fragrance to You, My King. Amen.

Handling Unwanted Attention

"Thou shalt hide them in the secret of thy presence from the pride of man: thou shalt keep them secretly in a pavilion from the strife of tongues."

Psalm 31:20

Lord God,

I look to you in navigating the complexities regarding attention and attraction. Ideally, my heart's desire would be to attract only the men with whom I have a romantic interest. But I know this is not a realistic expectation. While it's nice to feel desirable, it's disappointing when that attention comes from a man I do not desire. God, I pray that you will guide me in handling these situations with grace and integrity.

Lord, I also ask that You help me to have strength when an attractive, but ungodly, man approaches me. It's easy to want to take in that attention because they're attractive, but I don't want to feed my ego instead of my spirit. Help me to not fall prey to the attention of men who do not love You, Lord.

I want to guard my heart from leading anyone on unintentionally. I recognize the tendency to seek validation through attention, and if I'm not careful, I might cross boundaries without realizing it. Lord, help me to guard my heart and the hearts of others.

I trust You to guide me to the right person and, likewise, help me walk away from those who are not for me. I lean into Your Spirit for truth. In Jesus' Name, Amen.

Fostering Healthy Friendships

"Iron sharpeneth iron;
so a man sharpeneth the
countenance of his friend."

Proverbs 27:17

Dear God,

Love is beautiful. But this world seems to exalt romantic love above all other loves. Lord, help me not to miss out on enjoying and being grateful for the platonic love that is found in my friendships. I don't want to be so distracted by what I don't have that I miss what I do.

Would you strengthen me as a friend? Help me to be wise in my counsel, knowing when to speak and when to stay silent. I want to uplift my friends and encourage them towards a deeper relationship with You. I also want friends who will positively influence my life. I know that all of my relationships will impact me one way or another. I pray that Your Spirit will give me discernment in how I spend my time and emotions. I want to invest in friendships that will give me life!

Lord, I pray that You will bring friends into my life who are more spiritually mature than I am, because I know that will push me into greater obedience and maturity. Help me to be open to those I may not have considered before, such as individuals who are older than me or those who don't share the same interests. I want to be open to learning and growing with whoever You choose.

For my nonbelieving friends, I pray that You will use my life to help lead them to the truth. Give me the grace to shine Your light and not compromise. Help me to be open to who You want me to pour into, for your glory. In Jesus' Name, Amen.

Embracing Vulnerability in Relationships

"My power is made perfect in weakness."

2 Corinthians 12:9

Heavenly Father,

I recognize the significance of vulnerability in relationships, and I understand that suppressing my emotions isn't beneficial. I ask that You grant me the strength and courage, Lord, to confront these feelings, especially when they're tinged with anger and pain. I acknowledge that bottling up emotions isn't healthy, so I turn to You first, God, to release them through prayer. I trust You as the ultimate Healer and Guide.

Holy Spirit, lead me in discerning the appropriate level of sharing with others. I value vulnerability in nurturing connections and refuse to let fear hinder me. Guide me in finding a balance where I can express my feelings without overwhelming others, especially when I'm dealing with personal challenges.

Many of us grapple with knowing how to bring up instances when we've been hurt. Sometimes, there's a tendency to sweep these issues under the rug, but for the sake of healthy relationships, they must be addressed. Lord, please grant me the wisdom to process my negative emotions with You, so I can approach the person who has hurt me with grace and clarity.

God, I know that all these things will help me in my future relationships–not just with my spouse, but with friends and family. Help me to know how to be vulnerable with grace and truth. In Jesus' Name, Amen.

Dealing with Family Expectations

"Many are the plans in the mind of a man, but it is the purpose of the LORD that will stand".

Proverbs 19:21

Dear Lord,

Thank you for giving me a loving family. One that desires to see me happy and well-supported. I understand that some of them believe I would find greater fulfillment with a husband. However, I recognize that my ultimate source of joy is found in You, and You alone.

Whether I am married or not, You assure me of Your care through every season of life. I need not fear an uncertain future when I have the assurance of Your presence with me every step of the way.

Help me, Lord, to resist succumbing to anxiety when my family brings up the topic of marriage. Grant them the insight to see that my sufficiency lies in Christ. Although I desire marriage, may my reliance on You and Your perfect timing serve as a testament to my family. Enable me to offer them encouragement as I seek Your guidance and direction in my life.

Jesus, help me to also acknowledge that I have a family not only by blood but also through the Spirit. The Body of Christ comprises my extended family, where I find support, growth, and care. Help me (and my family) not to scorn or diminish the significance of these relationships simply because they do not include a spouse. Guide my heart toward gratitude and unwavering trust in You. Amen.

Overcoming Fear of Commitment

*"For God hath not given
us the spirit of fear; but of power,
and of love, and of a sound mind."*

2 Timothy 1:7

Dear God,

Marriage is a significant commitment, created by You as a lifelong, sacred covenant between two people. Entering into any exclusive relationship can feel like a big step.

In a world where divorce is common, it can be challenging to commit to someone for fear that they may leave. This can create tension and make the risk seem greater.

Lord, the thought of facing heartbreak in serious relationships can be daunting. It can lead to a desire to move slowly in order to avoid getting hurt. Yet, I understand that relationships require vulnerability and trust. Please grant me wisdom and maturity in navigating this.

Help me guard my heart in a way that still allows for meaningful connections. Help me to take life one day at a time, trusting that no matter what the future holds, You will provide the tools I need to persevere. When fear arises, may I remember Your power and presence, knowing that even in the midst of storms, You will never abandon me.

As I step into new relationships, help me to walk without fear, avoiding poor judgments and unhealthy attachment styles. Instill confidence in me, in You, and in Your ability to sustain me through all circumstances.
In Jesus' Name, Amen.

Seeking God's Guidance in Dating

"In all thy ways acknowledge him, and he shall direct thy paths."

Proverbs 3:6

Dear Lord,

There is so much information out there about dating. From strategies on how to attract a partner to recognizing red flags and signs of interest, sometimes it feels like what I see contradicts other advice I previously believed. With so many conflicting views, even within the Christian community, it's hard to know which to trust.

God, You know me. You know my personality, my hobbies, and my talents. You know exactly who I need to attract and partner with. I want to trust in Your guidance on how I should conduct myself when dating. Holy Spirit, please shatter any falsehoods I've been believing. Help me to not follow dating trends but to stand by what is tried and true. I don't want to mislead myself or hurt someone in the process of seeking a stable relationship.

Additionally, Lord, please help me with my timing. Sometimes I feel unsure about my role in the process, but I trust that "he who finds a wife finds a good thing." My time is Yours, God. I want to use it according to Your will. Help me discern how much to invest in dating in this season of my life.

I choose to let go of the pressure to figure everything out. I don't need to be an expert to enter a successful relationship. I have the Holy Spirit living in me, and I choose to believe that He will lead and guide me. Father, I know I'm not alone and that You're going to help me with every step. In Jesus' Name, Amen.

Building a Strong Relationship with God

*"Draw nigh to God, and
he will draw nigh to you.
Cleanse your hands, ye sinners;
and purify your hearts,
ye double minded."*

James 4:8

Dear Father,

I want my intentions in prayer to be pure. I come to You with my problems, doubts, and worries, like You ask me to. But I don't want to approach You simply because I know You have the power to solve my issues. I don't want to treat You like a genie, whose sole purpose is to serve me. No, I want to love You and be in a healthy relationship with You.

Lord, as I process my feelings about singleness and marriage, would You help my heart be molded closer to Yours? Prayer is communication between us, and I want to spend that time not just listing off requests but also hearing from You. Jesus, help me to intentionally pause and not rush through our time together.

Holy Spirit, would You ignite a fire in my heart for holy prayer? I want to spend time praying about the things that matter to You and will impact the world around me. I don't want to only approach You when I have wants, I want to be burdened by what others need intercession for! Lord, make my heart a house of prayer!

I want to weep over what makes You weep and rejoice over what You delight in. I want prayer to not only be a time when I share my heart with You but also when You share Your heart with me. Purify my intentions and help me to love You, Lord, as we communicate together.
In Your Name, Amen.

Addressing Financial Challenges

*"But my God shall
supply all your need according
to his riches in glory by Christ Jesus."*

Philippians 4:19

Dear God,

Fear often comes when I forget that You are my Provider. You tell me that You will supply all my needs, including my finances. At times, as a single woman, I crave the financial stability that marriage seems to offer. I sometimes fear what would happen if I lost my job. The economy is in constant flux, and many people seem worried. I would love to have a partner to weather the storm with and rely on.

However, I know that for some, marriage doesn't necessarily bring better financial security. Partners can have massive amounts of debt or mismanage money. So, Lord, please prepare my spouse to be someone with financial integrity who is a good worker. I want to be with a man who honors You and cares for his family with his finances.

Lord, even if I partner with a spouse who has incredible financial abilities, I know that only You have full control. Money can always be lost. You are the only true provider who will never fail. I want my trust to first be found in You! You are my Provider and will always be, whether I'm single or married. I trust in You. In Your Name, Amen.

Confronting the Fear of Remaining Single

"Fear not, for I am with you; be not dismayed, for I am your God; I will strengthen you, I will help you, I willuphold you with my righteous right hand."

Isaiah 41:10

Heavenly Father,

I do not have to be afraid. I *do not* have to fear. You tell me that You are the light of my life. Wherever I go, whether I'm single or married, You are the One who will give my life strength, purpose, and hope. Your love is the highest love I could ever experience, and with You, I lack nothing.

Father, You know I desire a husband. You know that staying single forever causes me fear. However, I refuse to be paralyzed or dragged down in my race by something that isn't yet a reality. I will walk by faith, not sight. I will live in the daily moment, seeing Your provision for me. I know that whatever I face, You will give me all I need to endure and glorify You.

When I do start to feel the ache of loneliness, Lord, would You comfort me with Your Spirit? I know You've used those in Your body to bring warmth and joy to my life. I pray that You will continue to lead me to individuals who will help uplift my spirits and turn my gaze towards You. You are the only One who will truly satisfy, and I want to be found in You, not wallowing in my fears over being single. Lord, I release my desire for the future to You. I refuse to let my relationship status dictate my joy in the Lord. I will rejoice in all seasons!
In Jesus' Name, Amen.

Finding Hope and Encouragement in God's Promises

*"May the God of hope fill
you with all joy and peace
as you trust in him, so that you
may overflow with hope
by the power of the Holy
Spirit."*

Romans 15:13

Lord Jesus,

You are the source of all peace. I know I can trust in Your promises to me—promises that You will never leave me, promises to support and uplift me, promises to forever love me. Why should I despair with You by my side? Your care for me is abundantly clear. I know whatever future I face will be filled with joy when I rely on You.

Holy Spirit, please help me to abound in hope. I want to be fruitful for the kingdom and produce an offering of praise for all You've done in my life and all I know You will do. Father, I thank You for all the blessings You've given me. And I thank You for all of my blessings yet to come. All of Your "no's" are for my good. Thank You for protecting me from stumbling by withholding certain gifts. Lord, I trust You to lead and guide.

Jesus, I'm believing that You will make a way for me to marry a devoted man of God. I'm coming to You in faith, knowing You have the authority and power to make anything happen. So, Lord, I'm praying that You will allow me to step into the gift of marriage. But until then, Father, You are still worthy of praise. Even while I wait, my life will hold deep meaning and purpose as I love, know, and serve You, my King. In Your Precious Name, Amen.